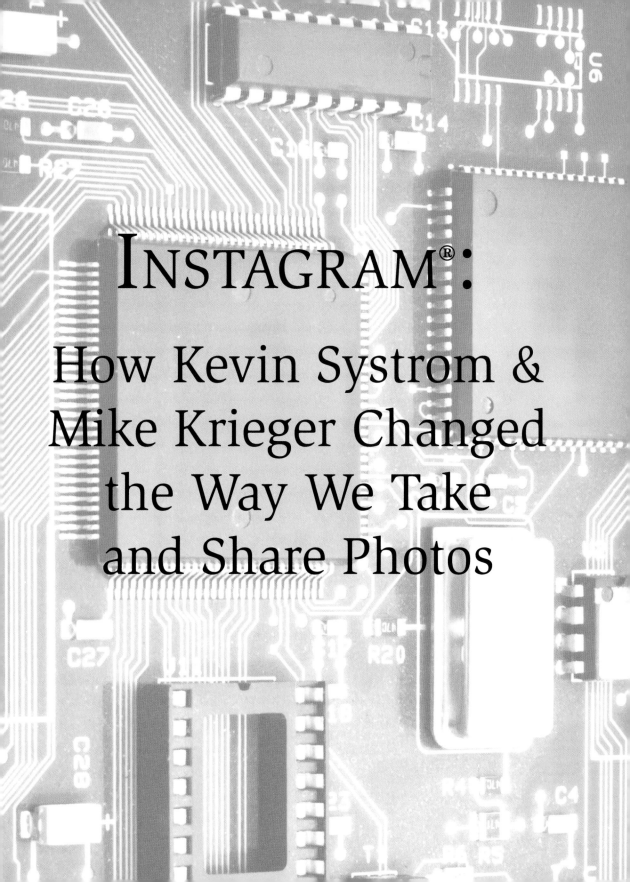

INSTAGRAM®:

How Kevin Systrom &
Mike Krieger Changed
the Way We Take
and Share Photos

WIZARDS OF TECHNOLOGY

WIZARDS OF TECHNOLOGY

INSTAGRAM®:

How Kevin Systrom & Mike Krieger Changed the Way We Take and Share Photos

ROSA WATERS

Mason Crest

Mason Crest
450 Parkway Drive, Suite D
Broomall, PA 19008
www.masoncrest.com

Printed and bound in the United States of America.

First printing
9 8 7 6 5 4 3 2 1

Series ISBN: 978-1-4222-3178-4
ISBN: 978-1-4222-3183-8
ebook ISBN: 978-1-4222-8719-4

Cataloging-in-Publication Data on file with the Library of Congress.

CONTENTS

KEY ICONS TO LOOK FOR:

Text-Dependent Questions: These questions send the reader back to the text for more careful attention to the evidence presented there.

Words to Understand: These words with their easy-to-understand definitions will increase the reader's understanding of the text, while building vocabulary skills.

Series Glossary of Key Terms: This back-of-the book glossary contains terminology used throughout this series. Words found here increase the reader's ability to read and comprehend higher-level books and articles in this field.

Research Projects: Readers are pointed toward areas of further inquiry connected to each chapter. Suggestions are provided for projects that encourage deeper research and analysis.

Sidebars: This boxed material within the main text allows readers to build knowledge, gain insights, explore possibilities, and broaden their perspectives by weaving together additional information to provide realistic and holistic perspectives.

Words to Understand

programming language: A type of computer code designed to be easily understood by humans.

colleagues: The people you work with.

entrepreneurs: People who start their own businesses, often taking financial risks to do so.

startups: New companies just starting out.

selective: Careful about who is chosen.

internships: Starting jobs to help young people gain experience.

retrospect: Looking back.

CHAPTER ONE

Experience Is Everything

On 12:15 a.m., October 6, 2010, Instagram went live. This was the moment Kevin Systrom and Mike Krieger and had worked so hard to reach. Exhausted but happy, they headed for bed. "We figured we'd have at least six hours before anyone discovered the app so we could grab some shut-eye," Kevin wrote on the company's blog.

But they were wrong. Within minutes, downloads began pouring in from all corners of the globe. Kevin and Mike were amazed—and overjoyed. After only a few hours, they had 10,000 users—and that number was still growing. "Are we counting wrong?" they asked each other.

At the end of the first week after the company's launch, Instagram had

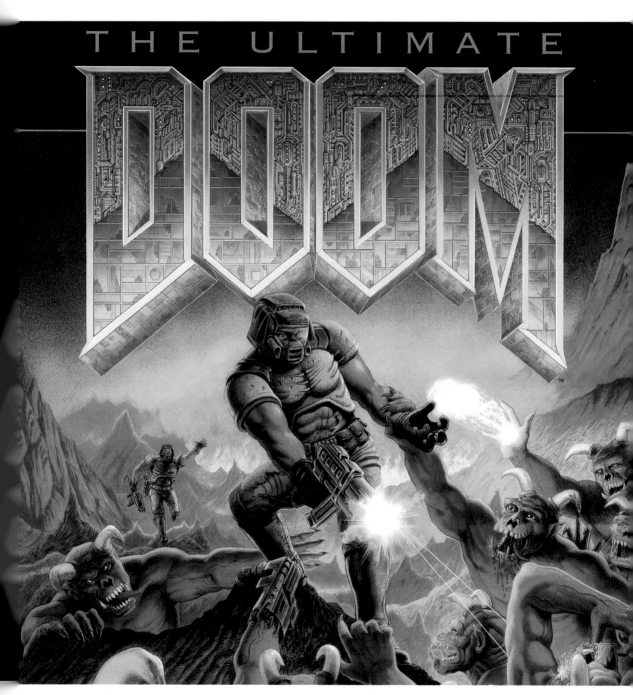

The video game *Doom II* was what first got Kevin interested in programming.

been downloaded 100,000 times. Another week passed, and another 100,000 people had downloaded the app. By the middle of December, the community had grown to a million users.

"We believe it's the beginning of something bigger," Kevin wrote on his blog. "It was both rewarding and humbling to see people embrace Instagram as both a new home on their iPhone—and a new way of communicating visually with people around the world. We believe this is only the beginning. With 6.7 billion people in the world, we're a tiny fraction of the way there, but we're extremely happy with the progress."

Kevin and Mike had come a long way in just a short time!

THEIR CHILDHOODS

Kevin Systrom began his life in Holliston, Massachusetts, on December 30, 1983. As a child, he often received very high scores in school and was known as a bright kid. Kevin's love for programming and computer languages began when he first had access to a computer in the home; he was twelve years old at the time.

Playing videogames was one of the ways Kevin enjoyed using the computer. A game known as *Doom II* interested him so much that he tried his hand at editing the different levels found in the game. "That was how I got into it, actually. I'll credit *Doom II* for everything," he said in an interview, referring to how he first began programming. His interest in programming did not end with *Doom II*, though.

The first computer ***programming language*** Kevin learned was QBasic, but he eventually moved on to more complex languages as his expertise grew. One program he wrote using Visual Basic allowed him to boot his friends offline when they were using American Online (AOL), a popular Internet browsing and social networking tool at the time. His online antics actually caused his family's AOL account to be banned! The Internet was Kevin's playground, and the expansion of the Internet only made him even more enthusiastic about the future.

Middlesex School gave Kevin a great educational foundation.

Make Connections: Networking

One of the greatest ways to get your idea out there is to share it with other people. Kevin and Mike had the pleasure of meeting a few very well-known people in the technological world through his time at Stanford and during his first internships. A few of the influential people he met were Sean Parker, one of the cofounders of Napster and first president of Facebook; Mark Zuckerberg, one of the cofounders of Facebook; and Adam D'Angelo, the Chief Technology Officer of Facebook. Knowing all these people would help Kevin and Mike get their idea for Instagram off the ground.

Kevin attended high school at Middlesex School, a boarding school located in Concord, Massachusetts, for students in grades nine through twelve. Many of the students stay at the school full-time, while only about a third are considered day students. It costs a lot to attend Middlesex School, but Kevin's parents had the money to give their son this educational opportunity. His mother, Diane, worked as a marketing executive, and his father, Douglas, was a president in a human resources position. They knew that students who graduate from Middlesex School are well-prepared for college life.

Classes are very small at the school to encourage students to get involved and stay interested in what they are learning. The unique attitude of the school allowed Kevin to replace a class he wasn't interested in—biology—with a different class that grabbed his attention: computer science. By the time he graduated, he was more than ready for the next step of his education. He had no difficulty being accepted into Stanford University.

Meanwhile, Mike Krieger had grown up in a very different area of the world. He was born on March 4, 1986, in São Paulo, Brazil. His birth name is Michel, but his friends and **colleagues** in the United States refer to him

Stanford University's location in California's Silicon Valley makes it an ideal place to get connected with the tech industry.

Make Connections: A Love of Photography

During Kevin's junior year of college, he traveled to Italy to study photography. He brought a very powerful SLR camera with him, but his teacher immediately swapped it with a less powerful camera. Kevin says this experience taught him "the beauty of vintage photography and also the beauty of imperfection."

as Mike. Mike moved to the United States in 2004 to continue his education as a student at Stanford University. And that's where he and Kevin first met.

STANFORD UNIVERSITY

One of the reasons Stanford University has attracted so many young *entrepreneurs* is because of its convenient location. Stanford, California, is part of a larger area known as Silicon Valley, where many technological *startups* begin. Some of the brightest minds have studied and graduated from this well-known university.

Make Connections: Silicon Valley

"Silicon Valley" is the nickname given to a region in northern California. It's home to many of the world's largest technology corporations, as well as thousands of small startups. The nickname started in the 1970s because of the many manufacturers of silicon chips (used in computers and other electronic devices) that were located there. Today, Silicon Valley continues to be a center for high-tech businesses.

Odeo would go on to have a large role in the creation of Twitter, one of the most successful social media companies in the world. Working at the company was an excellent experience for Kevin.

Despite Kevin's interest in computer programming, he didn't actually earn a computer science degree. Instead, he majored in management science and engineering; in fact, he only took one computer science class at the university. According to Kevin, he didn't get a very good grade in the class, and he had to work very hard to earn it. He focused his attention on engineering, instead. "Stanford is one of the best places to meet engineers who are extremely smart but also well-rounded," he said in an interview.

Kevin's management classes got him interested in starting his own company, and he gained valuable experience during his time at Stanford. He was selected to be a part of the Mayfield Fellows, a very **selective** program for students looking to get involved in growing technology companies. Only about a dozen students are accepted into the program, which helps those students find **internships** and future jobs in companies both large and small.

One of the first companies Kevin interned at was Odeo, which eventually reformed as a new company that developed Twitter after Kevin left. According to Kevin, "Experience is everything," and interning at Odeo was a great way to teach him how startup companies worked. Mike was learning a lot as well. "We both had really amazing internships then," Kevin said, "that got us to get interested in entrepreneurship and get excited about doing it when we got out."

Mike totally agreed. "A day on the job was worth a year of experience," he said, "and what happens is the collection of experiences and knowledge you can get from those sources are super important."

Working at Odeo gave Kevin the opportunity to meet Mark Zuckerberg, who offered Kevin a job at Facebook in 2006. Kevin turned down the offer so that he would have time finish his degree at Stanford. "I'm sure in **retrospect** it would have been a nice deal, but it's funny where you end up," Kevin said in an interview with *Forbes*. Instead of working for one successful social networking website, Kevin ended up creating his own!

craigslist

US   Canada   Europe   Asia/Pacific/Middle East   Oceania   Latin America   Africa

a

burn
mingham
than
rence / muscle shoals
dsden-anniston
ntsville / decatur
bile
ntgomery
scaloosa

chorage / mat-su
banks
nai peninsula
utheast alaska

gstaff / sedona
have county
oenix
scott
ow low
rra vista
son
ma

s

etteville
smith

Idaho

boise
east idaho
lewiston / clarkston
twin falls

Illinois

bloomington-normal
champaign urbana
chicago
decatur
la salle co
mattoon-charleston
peoria
rockford
southern illinois
springfield
western IL

Indiana

bloomington
evansville
fort wayne
indianapolis
kokomo
lafayette / west lafayette
muncie / anderson
richmond
south bend / michiana
terre haute

Missouri

columbia / jeff city
joplin
kansas city
kirksville
lake of the ozarks
southeast missouri
springfield
st joseph
st louis

Montana

billings
bozeman
butte
great falls
helena
kalispell
missoula
montana (old)

Nebraska

grand island
lincoln
north platte
omaha / council bluffs
scottsbluff / panhandle

Nevada

elko

Pennsylvania

altoona-johnstows
cumberland valley
erie
harrisburg
lancaster
lehigh valley
meadville
philadelphia
pittsburgh
poconos
reading
scranton / wilkes-
state college
williamsport
york

Rhode Island

rhode island

South Carolina

charleston
columbia
florence
greenville / upstate
hilton head
myrtle beach

South Dakota

One of Kevin's early projects was similar to Craigslist, a website where people can post items they want to buy or sell from other users.

Make Connections: Hobbies

Mike worked very hard, but he also found time to pursue some hobbies outside of school and work. He worked on an Internet radio station while he was attending Stanford University, and even performed as a DJ in his spare time.

During his years at Stanford, Kevin also started a few personal projects. One of his first startups was a website similar to Craigslist, except it specifically targeted people attending Stanford University. Students could use the website to buy and trade items. This Craigslist competitor eventually gained over 8,000 members, which wasn't bad for a service built by someone who didn't even have a computer science degree!

Meanwhile, Mike was working on his own area of expertise. His major was symbolic systems, with a specific focus in human-computer interaction. He was most interested in how humans used computers both in the present time and how they might use them in the future, and that interest has never gone away. Mike interned at a few well-known companies including Microsoft and Foxmarks, where his skills as a software developer went to great use. Mike was learning how larger companies worked, while Kevin continued working at and observing small startups.

FIRST JOBS

Kevin wasted no time finding a job after graduating from college. His first job was at Google, where he stayed for two years. His marketing experience from his internships helped him earn the title of Associate Product Marketing Manager. Some of the projects he worked on were Gmail, Google Reader, Google Calendar, Google Docs and Spreadsheets. All these applications helped Google users become more connected with each other while using the Internet.

Text-Dependent Questions

1. What was the first problem Kevin and Mike encountered after officially launching Instagram?
2. When did Kevin first start dabbling with computer programming?
3. List two computer programming languages that Kevin learned as a child.
4. According to the author, why does Stanford University attract so many young entrepreneurs? Explain.
5. What did Mike mean when he said, "A day on the job was worth a year of experience?"

During his time at Google, Kevin says he learned "how to talk about products," which would become a very important skill down the road when he was looking for funding for Instagram! Kevin wasn't allowed to join the programming team due to his lack of a computer science degree, so he took on a new position as part of the corporate development team after a year of working at Google. During his time on the team, he worked directly with the various startups that Google was acquiring, which inspired him to want to start his own company one day. If he was lucky, he reasoned, Google would take an interest in his startup, too.

Kevin couldn't resist getting involved. "I saw so many entrepreneurs having tons of fun starting companies, that I jumped to a company started by some Googlers," he said. That company was known as Nextstop, which was later acquired by Facebook. Kevin began in the new company's marketing department, but he eventually took on a job as an engineer. This was the moment he says he truly became a programmer. "Only at my next job at Nextstop would I say I went from being a hobbyist to being able to write code that would go into production," he explained.

Research Project

 At first, Kevin considered his interest in programming to be merely a hobby. A hobby, though, is something that gets us excited, so our hobbies can sometimes point us toward good career choices. What are you favorite hobbies? Do some research. What jobs would give you a chance to get paid for doing your hobby? What education and experience would you need to be qualified for these jobs?

Mike followed a slightly different path from Kevin's. Rather than jumping straight into the work force, he continued his studies at Stanford University and eventually earned a master's degree. After graduation, he joined an instant-messaging firm known as Meebo. He worked there as an engineer for a year and a half.

And now the time had come: Mike and Kevin were ready to join forces to start their own company.

Words to Understand

prototype: The first version of a product that is made, to be used as an example.

CHAPTER TWO

Inspiration
for Instagram

bout a year into working for Nextstop, Kevin began thinking about his own startup project. In order to be successful, he would have to hone his skills as a programmer first. "While I was there working in marketing, I started doing more and more engineering at night on simple ideas that helped me learn how to program," he explained. "One of these ideas was combining elements of Foursquare with the elements of Mafia Wars." This combination would become Burbn.

Both Foursquare and Mafia Wars were applications that could be used on a mobile device. Foursquare used mobile technology to allow a user to "check in" to places they visited in exchange for rewards. A person who checked in to a local coffee shop might receive a coupon for a discounted coffee, for example. Mafia Wars was a multiplayer game

Mike and Kevin wanted their new app to be able to connect easily to Facebook, the social networking giant.

that also functioned as a social network. Players could collect items and compete against each other, all from their mobile devices. Burbn would combine these functions into one app.

Kevin began working on this project alone, relying on his friends and colleagues to test it. "I figured I could build a **prototype** of the idea in HTML5 and get it to some friends," he explained. HTML5 is another type of computer programming language. The first version of the Burbn application had no branding or design at all. It was just a functioning application.

While Kevin was working on Burbn, he realized he needed help to truly improve his application. "At a party," he said, "I ran into a bunch of people who would basically make starting Burbn a reality. At that party were two people from Baseline Ventures and Andreessen Horowitz. I showed the prototype, and we decided we'd meet up for coffee and talk about it."

At this point, Kevin was still working for Nextstop, but he knew if he wanted to give Burbn the attention it deserved, he needed to focus on it completely. "I decided to take the drive and leave my job to go solo and see if Burbn could be a company. Within two weeks of leaving, I raised $500,000 from both Baseline and Andreessen Horowitz, and started working on finding a team," he explained. Going to that party was one of the best moves Kevin ever made!

BURBN, INC.

Kevin Systrom found a business partner in Mike Krieger, who was very interested in the idea of building an application together. Having an extra person on his team allowed Kevin to get some real feedback about what was working with the application and what was not. With Mike's guidance and the funding they had received, Burbn began to take shape.

Using the application, users could check in to locations (similar to Foursquare), make plans (to check in to locations later), earn points (by

Instagram (Hefe filter) ↑

← Smartphone camera

Kevin and Mike figured out a way that Instagram could make phone photos look much better using filters.

hanging out with friends and checking in to locations together), and post pictures. Unfortunately, there was just too much to work with. "It felt cluttered, and overrun with features," Kevin explained. Foursquare was also immensely popular, so it would be difficult for Burbn to compete against it.

Any good business owner needs to learn to make tough decisions. That's what Kevin and Mike had to do now. "It was really difficult to decide to start from scratch," Kevin said, "but we went out on a limb, and basically cut everything in the Burbn app except for its photo, comment, and like capabilities. What remained was Instagram."

The reason Kevin and Mike chose to narrow down the application to just photos was because that was the feature most testers liked when they used the original Burbn app. The name of their new app came from a combinations of two words: "instant" and "telegram." Kevin and Mike wanted to emphasize the fact that the images were uploaded almost instantly and could be used as a way to communicate between one person and another. According to Kevin, another reason he liked the word Instagram is because "it also sounded camera-y!"

SOLVING PROBLEMS

Kevin and Mike were great problem solvers. They thought of issues that might arise before they even happened. During a speech he gave at Stanford University, Kevin outlined a few problems they addressed long before Instagram went live.

The first problem they wanted to address was that "mobile photos don't look so great." He explained, "We've all had that experience . . . you're seeing the sunset, you take a snapshot, and it looks washed out, you can barely see the sun, etcetera. And we were like, 'That's the major problem we want to solve.'"

Kevin and Mike couldn't do anything about the quality of photos being taken by mobile phones, but they could help users make their photos look better. They introduced filters as a way to edit photos without users needing any sort of photo-editing expertise. All users needed to do to apply a filter was click it in the Instagram menu. There were all sorts of filters, ranging from different color tones to grayscale possibilities. Users loved this feature, which completely solved the first problem Kevin and Mike had noticed.

The second problem Kevin mentioned during his speech was that "uploads on mobile phones take a really long time." The way Kevin and Mike got around that problem was by starting uploads while a user was still typing in a caption. They also decreased the time it took to upload a

Kevin's friendship with Jack Dorsey, one of Twitter's founders, was a big help in Instagram's early days.

More and more users were signing up, ready to "Create and Share the World's Moments."

photo by reducing the photo size before it was uploaded. Like the addition of filters, the solution Kevin and Mike found to the second problem made users very happy. When they pressed "done" after entering their caption, the image had already finished uploading.

The third and final problem Kevin spoke about was that they "really wanted to allow you to share out to multiple services at once." They felt people would be more likely to use Instagram if it were connected to the other social networking websites. He explained, "We felt like, should you have to make the decision of taking a photo with a Facebook app, the Twitter app, so on and so on, or should you just take it in one place and distribute it to many places at once?"

Make Connections: Social Media Networks

At the time of Instagram's release, two social media websites were already dominating the Internet. Facebook, a website which began as a way to connect college students, had by this time expanded to millions of users around the globe. Twitter, the micro-blogging platform, allowed people to communicate using short snippets of text. For Instagram to be successful, it needed to introduce something new to the world of social media. Facebook had always allowed its users to upload photos, but the website did not solely focus on that functionality. Instagram was launched with an emphasis on sharing photos and posting comments. It wasn't until later that video functionality was added.

INSTANT SUCCESS

Kevin and Mike did everything they could to think of every possible scenario before Instagram launched to ensure that it had a fair shot at becoming popular with its users. Kevin truly believed in the app before it went live. He said in an interview that he knew it would be successful from day one of its release. He recalls, "I literally remember looking to my side, to my cofounder Mike, and being like, 'I think this thing is going to be big.'" Within just a few hours of its launch, he realized he was right!

As the website and application grew, Kevin and Mike struggled to keep up with the new demands of the company. Through it all, Kevin remained humble. "I had never seen people fall in love with something so quickly. And I'm not going to take credit," he said later, "and I'm not going to say that we knew exactly what we were doing, but we just hit all the right elements at the right time and then we were like, 'Okay, let's capture this, and let's make it even better.'"

One of the reasons Kevin and Mike knew what users would like is because they tested the application extensively before officially releasing it. "In order to test whether you're working on the right thing or not, you need to put it in front of people," Kevin said. This testing started long before Instagram was even created, and actually began with the first versions of Burbn.

The earliest users of Burbn were confused by all of its features. "We would be in a busy bar and trying to explain to them on our mobile phones and they just wouldn't get it," Kevin recalls. "And that happened enough in front of people outside of our friend group that it was really clear we had to work on something different. Or at least refine the idea." Fortunately, Instagram was different enough to be successful. Users didn't become confused by the clutter that was in the original Burbn app.

INCREDIBLE GROWTH

The development of Instagram began in early 2010. It took Kevin and Mike a total of seven months to completely finish developing Instagram. When it was finally released later that year, they were the only two people working for their company. They needed to hire more people to help out.

The first new person to join the project was Shayne Sweeney, who

Research Project

As companies grow, so do their needs. Instagram began in a very small office, but eventually moved to what had been Twitter's original office. Using the Internet, research the size of Instagram now. How many employees work for Instagram now? Is the company still hiring? Go to its website and see if it has any job listings. Do any of them look interesting to you? What education and experiences would you need to qualify for these jobs?

worked as an engineer. Jessica Zollman was brought in about ten months after that as a community evangelist. She focused on listening to the community and bringing those needs back to the developers so that they could improve Instagram as a whole.

Mike admits, "I don't really remember the first two months of our startup because we didn't sleep, and I think short-term memory goes out of the way." Losing sleep is not uncommon for people involved in startup companies. Startups make very little money at the beginning of their existence, forcing the people working for those companies to work extra hard. Kevin and Mike did everything they could to ensure Instagram's success. As Mike puts it, "We put in a lot of late nights that were all about saying, 'What do we need to do to get our products to a place where people can keep using it, get excited about it, scale to the challenge?'"

All the expansion Instagram was doing required more office space. At about this time, Twitter's original headquarters, originally used by Odeo, was up for grabs. "After my internship with the Odeo folks, I used to go visit them at that office. So when the opportunity arose, I figured we should jump on it," Kevin explained. Instagram took the office space and moved everything into its new home.

Meanwhile, one of the biggest problems Instagram faced came from how fast it was expanding. The servers hosting the Instagram application and website could not handle all the traffic they were experiencing. One of the benefits of knowing so many successful tech innovators is that you have someone to call when you need help!

Kevin had met Adam D'Angelo, the chief technology officer of Facebook, at a party long before Instagram launched. When Kevin didn't know what to do about Instagram's servers crashing, he called Adam. "Adam spent thirty minutes on the phone with us just walking us through the basic things we needed to do to get back up," Kevin explained. "Those little events are the things that matter." Without Adam's help, Kevin and Mike would have had a much harder time getting the servers back online at such a pivotal point in Instagram's existence.

With that problem solved, they were ready for their new company to grow even bigger!

Words to Understand

policy: Established rule for how to do something.

priority: The thing considered to be the most important.

profits: Money that you make after paying off all expenses.

private: Owned by a few people, instead of having anyone able to buy shares.

evolve: Change as time goes on.

innovative: Having to do with a creative, new way of doing things.

perks: Benefits to doing something.

targeting: Trying to reach a certain person or thing.

CHAPTER THREE

Keeping Up

nstagram grew to have over one million registered users by the end of 2010, just four months after it was officially released to the public. The company hit another milestone in June of 2011 when it reached five million users. By September of that same year, the number of users doubled to ten million. In April of 2012, Instagram announced that it now had over thirty million users. A month later, Instagram announced that fifty-eight photographs were being uploaded and a new user was joining the service every second. The app's growth seemed limitless!

Although Instagram was blossoming, Kevin and Mike were still having some problems with the business aspect of the company. "It's not just

Kevin Systrom and Mike Krieger accept their Webby Breakout of the Year Award in 2012. The award honors excellence on the Internet.

about having a great idea," Kevin explained. "It's finding the people to bring in to make that idea happen and supporting them by shielding them from the press and the checking accounts that you have to set up, etcetera . . . especially raising capital. That can be a huge time sink."

Working on the application itself is only one part of what the company was doing. The rest of the company's time, money, and energy were spent working on things the public never sees. Financing, taxes, and laws can take up a lot of a startup company's time.

Despite that, Kevin and Mike made sure the company kept its creative focus. They worked hard to keep Instagram going strong. They knew the best way to do this was by introducing new features and listening to feedback from users.

CONNECTING USERS

One of Instagram's new features was hashtags. Twitter first popularized these special markers, used to organize posts into different categories, back in 2009. All hashtags begin with a pound symbol—#—and end with a word. One example of a hashtag would be: #hashtag.

Hashtags allow users to communicate with each other in a simpler way, and they held a special meaning when used on Instagram. People attending the same event could put a hashtag on their posts and then click on it to look at all other posts with the same hashtag. Clicking on the hashtag #newyears2015, for example, would bring up pictures that other users had tagged as having to do with that particular topic. It might include pictures of fireworks, New Year's parties, or anything to do with that event.

Instagram also made its application more widely available. Until 2012, Instagram was only available on iPhones. Instagram introduced an Android version of the application in April of 2012. The launch of Instagram for Android is what helped Instagram reach thirty million users that month.

Facebook's Mark Zuckerberg made Kevin and Mike an offer they couldn't refuse!

Despite the number of users, only thirteen employees were working for Instagram in 2012, many of them graduates from Stanford. These were people who were all devoted to their jobs. They had to be! Kevin had a *policy* that required all engineers working for the company to have a computer on them at all times. Kevin followed his own rule too. "It's our baby," he admitted. "It keeps us up and night and wakes us up in the morning." Sometimes he needed to interrupt a dinner at a restaurant to fix a problem with Instagram's servers.

Kevin and Mike were totally focused on Instagram's success—but that didn't meant that they made money their *priority*. In fact, they didn't define success using *profits*. "I think not focusing on money makes you sane," Kevin said in an interview. "In the long run, it can probably drive you crazy." Many investors wanted to buy Instagram, but Kevin turned them all down. This was still his baby. But then, later in 2012, Kevin was presented with an opportunity that was too good to pass up.

FACEBOOK BUYS INSTAGRAM

Kevin's old friend Jack Dorsey, one of Twitter's founders, made an offer to Kevin—but Kevin turned him down. He told Jack that he and Mike weren't interested in selling, that they wanted to remain a *private* company. When Facebook's Mark Zuckerberg made an offer, Kevin and Mike told him the same thing.

But Mark Zuckerberg wasn't going to take no as Kevin and Mike's final answer. On Easter weekend, he sent Kevin a text, inviting him to come over and discuss options. By the end of the weekend, Mark and Kevin had cut a deal. Mark Zuckerberg doubled Twitter's offer and agreed to buy Instagram for more than $730 million in cash and stock.

Jack Dorsey was upset. "I found out about the deal when I got to work and one of my employees told me about it," he said. "So I was heartbroken, since I did not hear from Kevin at all. We exchanged e-mails once

Despite all the changes going on with Instagram, users continued to use it for their photos.

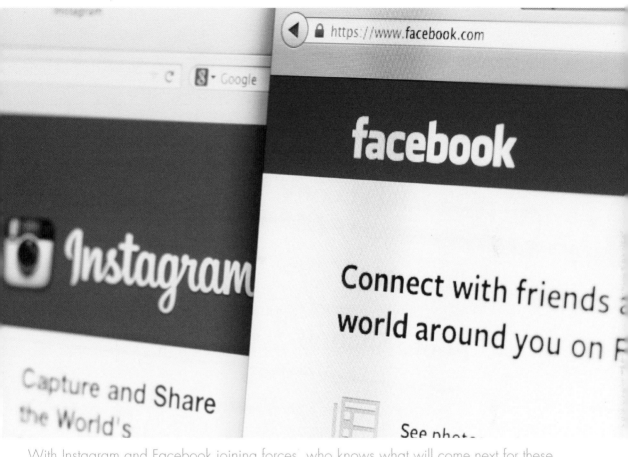

With Instagram and Facebook joining forces, who knows what will come next for these companies?

or twice, and I have seen him at parties. But we have not really talked at all since then, and that's sad."

Kevin says he didn't mean to snub Dorsey, though. "I'm not sure what changed my mind," he said in an interview with a writer for *Vanity Fair* magazine, "but Mark presented an entire plan of action. . . . It turns out that some of the biggest decisions get made relatively quickly, without much fanfare."

Instagram lost many users to competitor Flickr.com when users became angry over Instagram's rules about selling user photos.

Make Connections: Direct

Instagram introduced a feature known as Direct in December of 2013. This special service gave users a way to send images directly to one another without actually posting them on the website. It added a level of privacy that had not existed before, and served as a way for users to message each other without other people seeing what they were saying.

At the time, it was the largest buyout Facebook had ever made. Kevin, who didn't care so much about money as he did about making sure Instagram continued to move in the right direction, was told that he would continue to have some control over the company. "It's important to be clear that Instagram is not going away," he reassured users after the buyout was announced. "We'll be working with Facebook to *evolve* Instagram and build the network. We'll continue to add new features to the product and find new ways to create a better mobile photos experience."

MAKING MISTAKES

Every company makes mistakes, and Kevin and Mike made a very big mistake in December of 2012. The social networking website updated its policy to give itself the right to sell any photos uploaded to the website to third parties without notifying the users who uploaded those photos in the first place. This stirred a lot of controversy, with *National Geographic* magazine and Kim Kardashian being among the loudest voices to complain.

As a result of the policy change, many users threatened to leave Instagram to join a different photo-sharing website, such as Pheed and Flickr. Those websites gained a lot of new users the week Instagram introduced the new policy. A day later, Kevin told users, "Our intention in updating

Like Facebook, Instagram kept its successful mobile app free to use, but included advertisements to help the company make money from the free app.

the terms was to communicate that we'd like to experiment with ***innovative*** advertising that feels appropriate on Instagram. Instead it was interpreted by many that we are going to sell your photos to others without any compensation. That is not true."

Kevin continued his apology: "It is our mistake that this language is confusing. To be clear: it is not our intention to sell your photos. We are working on updated language in the terms to make this clear." Instagram eventually did introduce advertising, but it was not in the way users feared.

ADVERTISING

Instagram is free to use, but it requires a lot of money to run! At first, Instagram focused on growth by gaining funding through investors and companies. Early on, Kevin said he was "focused solely on the product and establishing ourselves as the leader in the mobile space," but he did admit he was looking at possible ways to make money in the future.

One of the ideas Kevin mentioned was the thought of offering a paid premium service, which would include **perks** such as extra filters not available through free accounts. This did not happen, though. A year after Facebook bought Instagram, the social media giant announced that it would be hosting advertising on Instagram in addition to Facebook.

Advertisements are one of the ways websites can make money. The main difference between the ads being displayed on Facebook and the ads that would be displayed on Instagram was the device that would be used. Most of Instagram's 150 million users access the website using a mobile device. Instagram sent out an announcement saying that it would be embracing advertising, starting in October of 2013, forcing mobile users to adjust to this change.

As usual, Instagram spoke up to tell users they had nothing to worry about regarding this new change. "Our aim is to make any advertisements

Text-Dependent Questions

1. What problems were Kevin and Mike having with the business aspect of the company when Instagram began to rise in popularity?
2. What are hashtags and how did they improve the Instagram experience?
3. What were Kevin and Mike given in return for selling Instagram?
4. What mistake did Instagram make in 2012 that greatly upset users?
5. Why were advertisements added to Instagram in 2013?

you see feel as natural to Instagram as the photos and videos many of you already enjoy from your favorite bands," the company wrote on its blog. "After all, our team doesn't just build Instagram, we use it each and every day."

The developers of the company would have to look at the ads being shown on the website too; they wanted to make sure the advertisements being displayed were appropriate for every user that looked at them. Fortunately, there is an option to hide ads that users do not want to see, although there is no way to get rid of the ads completely.

Using advertising as a way to make money is certainly not uncommon. Some of the most popular websites now using advertisements are Facebook, Twitter, Tumblr, YouTube, and Pinterest. Advertisements are now more effective at *targeting* specific users than ever before because websites can collect information about users in order to personalize the ads. Someone who frequently looks at pictures of automobiles on Instagram might be interested in car commercials, for example.

Trends tend to move from one website to another in such an interconnected world. Hashtags and the introduction of advertising are just two

Research Project

This chapter explored some of the ways Instagram has changed over the years. List the features outlined in this chapter and explain how they improved the overall Instagram experience. Then, research new features that have been added since 2013. How has Instagram adapted to the trends of other websites that are on the rise? Are there any websites currently competing directly with Instagram?

examples that affected Instagram directly. Instagram must continue to pay attention to its competitors if it is going to stay as successful as it is now. Facebook, on the other hand, will need to be careful not to force Instagram to become something the users will not like. Only time will tell what the future will look like for Instagram now that it's part of Facebook.

Words to Understand

wearables: Devices that you wear, instead of carry around.
revolutionize: Change in a big way.
media: A form of mass communication, such as music or videos.
credible: Trustworthy.
relevant: Still mattering.
obsessed: Constantly thinking about one thing.

CHAPTER FOUR

Instagram's Future

nstagram has come very far, but Kevin has still more goals for his app. Getting bought by Facebook hasn't changed that! He hopes that Instagram will eventually become the sole image-sharing application on every single type of mobile device, but he does not want to stop there. "We will be everywhere—on every platform, on every kind of phone and tablet and on **wearables**, which will be the core component of sharing," he said. As technology improves, so will the options available to Instagram users.

One of the newest pieces of technology which might help Instagram grow is Google Glass. Worn directly on the head, users can take

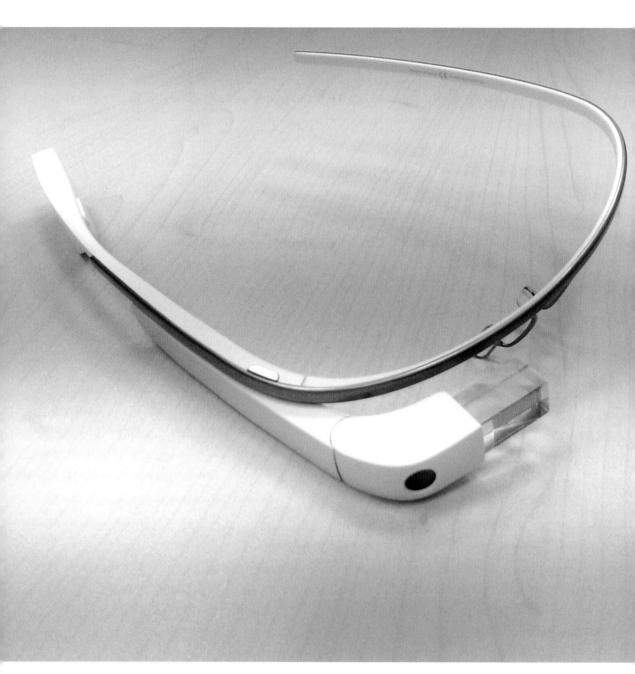

Google's newest invention, Google Glass, offers new opportunities to Instagram.

snapshots with literally just the blink of an eye. Photos can be taken in real time without the need of a handheld device. This would completely *revolutionize* the way people share visual *media*, whether it be in photo or video form.

The future of Instagram would involve more than just social media, however. "In five years," Kevin said, "I want to see not just content from my friends but my morning news on Instagram, from multiple channels." While Instagram was originally about encouraging users to be creative and connect with one another directly, he hopes it will become a more *credible* source of information. "I want Instagram to be the place I learn about the world."

EXPANDING TO VIDEO

Adding new features is how Instagram can stay *relevant* in an ever-changing world. One of the newest features Instagram added in 2013 is the ability to upload videos. These videos are restricted to fifteen seconds, so they must be short and to the point. Some other social media websites have offered the option to upload short videos, including Twitter's Vine, so adding videos is Instagram's way of keeping up.

Make Connections: Better Security

Social media websites must do a lot to ensure that its users stay protected. Accounts can be hacked or even duplicated against someone's will. Facebook and Instagram now require accounts that may have violated one of the website's rules to prove their identity through the use of photo identification.

You know you're successful when your face is on the cover of *Forbes* magazine!

Kevin Systrom is recognized as an expert in startups, and he's a frequent guest speaker at conferences. Here, Kevin (far right) is on a panel at a 2012 TechCrunch conference.

Instagram still focuses on what it does best. "Our goal is not to just be a photo-sharing app, but to be the way you share your life when you're on the go," Kevin said in an interview shortly after Instagram launched. Instagram's mission statement still remains very much the same.

Phone technology is constantly improving. Data transfer speeds get better and more affordable every year. It is only a matter of time before

Kevin holds his award at the 2013 Crunchie Awards hosted by tech website TechCrunch, just one of the amazing awards Systrom and Instagram have won.

Instagram hopes users will have as much fun recording and sharing video as they have sending photos to friends and family.

sending large video files will be a realistic possibility. Instagram is making sure it is prepared for when that happens!

AWARDS

Instagram has received a lot of attention over the years, starting with being named a runner-up for "Best Mobile App" for 2010 by TechCrunch. Kevin has been given a lot of attention of his own, starting with being named one of the "100 Most Creative People in Business in 2011" by Fast Company. He was listed as number sixty-six.

Both Kevin Systrom and Mike Krieger were included in *Inc.*'s "30 Under 30" list for their involvement in the creation of Instagram. *San*

Instagram's award-winning smartphone app helped make the company the success it is today.

Francisco Weekly acknowledged Instagram's roots by naming it the "Best Locally Made App" in its September 2011 Web Awards. Kevin and Mike were featured on the cover of *7x7Magazine*'s "The Hot 20 2011" issue. Kevin's face was also on *Forbes* magazine.

One of the most prestigious awards Instagram won, however, was being named Apple's "App of the Year" in 2011. The company that makes the iPhone currently hosts over a million different apps, and those numbers are growing every day. According to Apple, Instagram makes it "impossible to take a bad shot."

ADVICE

Kevin learned most of what he knows about startups by getting out there and just doing it. It is no surprise that his advice to future entrepreneurs is very much the same. "If you've got an idea, start today," he urges. "There's no better time than now to get going." Yet he tells people to be cautious, too. " That doesn't mean quit your job and jump into your idea 100 percent from day one, but there's always small progress that can be made to start the movement." Kevin waited several months before diving into Instagram completely.

When asked about the greatest challenge he faced when starting Instagram, he mentions his previous job. "Leaving a job with great people to start a company was the biggest challenge," he said. "It was a tough decision, but honestly I can't imagine doing it any other way." A person who wants to get involved in a startup has to commit to it completely at some point.

Mike Krieger has some advice of his own. In a speech, he told future entrepreneurs that they really need to be interested in what they are doing. It can't just feel like any other job. "It should be that you wake up and you're ***obsessed*** with this idea and you want to make it happen," he explained. "Only when you have the drive to push forward will you truly succeed."

Continuing your education, even outside of school, is a good way to

Instagram helps Kevin and Mike share their passion for photography with millions of people around the world who can take and share beautiful photos with Instagram.

Research Project

Instagram is a service that is directly affected by the technology available at the time. Mobile devices such as smartphones, tablets, and Google Glass are all realistic ways to take and upload media to Instagram. Using the Internet, research one new piece of technology that may be useful for Instagram users. How will it change the way Instagram evolves over the next few years?

stay ahead of the competition. "We built all of the initial version of Instagram ourselves," Mike said, "from things we mostly just were self-taught in." Neither Mike nor Kevin earned degrees in computer programming, and they needed to ask for a lot of help along the way. They weren't afraid to ask!

INSPIRATION

Kevin and Mike are creators, and that likely won't ever change. They're still too young, though, to predict what their next moves will be professionally. Maybe they'll stick with Instagram for years to come. Or maybe they'll create something brand new, either together or separately. Either way, they're sure to be at the forefront of the tech world.

One of the greatest things that inspires Kevin, he says, are "people who spend their days creating—whether that be in technology or otherwise. I'm always in awe of people who are artists in their fields—people who understand that simply by taking ideas and translating them into reality, they've created value in the world."

Instagram allows artists to be creative, and that is exactly what inspired Kevin to work as hard as he did. "It was a humble vision back

Text-Dependent Questions

1. What new invention might help Instagram grow in popularity? Why?
2. Why did Instagram introduce video in 2013, and why will its use likely increase over the years?
3. What award did Instagram win from Apple in 2011 and why is it such a big deal?
4. What advice does Kevin Systrom have for future entrepreneurs?
5. What does Mike say about how interested a person should be when working for a startup company?

when we started," he said, "simply to work with a talented group of people who share the same passion for mobile photography that Mike and I do. Now, it's clear we've been presented with an opportunity to do something very big and improve the way the world communicates and shares in the real world. We work tirelessly to create the tools to achieve this goal."

After just a few years, Kevin and Mike have accomplished what they set out to do: they have connected the world in a new way. Users can go anywhere, take a picture, and easily share it with their friends with the click of a button. Rather than texting a friend that you saw something interesting, you can actually show them! Instagram has become a whole new level of social networking that bridges the gap between the Internet and the real world through the use of photography.

And it all started because two friends had a good idea—and worked hard to make it a reality.

FIND OUT MORE

In Books

Miles, Jason. *Instagram Power: Build Your Brand and Rearch More Customers with the Power of Pictures.* New York: McGraw-Hill, 2014.

Neher, Krista. *Visual Social Marketing for Dummies.* Hoboken, NJ: John Wiley & Sons, 2014.

Piscione, Deborah P. *Secrets of Silicon Valley.* New York: Palgrave Macmillan, 2013.

Taulli, Tom. *How to Create the next Facebook: Seeing Your Startup Through, from Idea to IPO.* New York: Apress, 2012.

Topper, Hilary. *Everything You Ever Wanted to Know about Social Media, but Were Afraid to Ask.* Bloomington, IN: Iuniverse, 2009.

On the Internet

Achieving Overnight Success: Kevin Systrom
joel.is/post/22436341176/achieving-overnight-success-kevin-systrom

The Genesis of Instagram
www.quora.com/Instagram/What-is-the-genesis-of-Instagram

Instagram's Kevin Systrom: The Stanford Billionaire Machine Strikes Again
www.forbes.com/sites/stevenbertoni/2012/08/01/instagrams-kevin-systrom-the-stanford-millionaire-machine-strikes-again

Kevin Systrom, Instagram's Man of Vision
www.theguardian.com/technology/2013/oct/11/instagram-kevin-systrom-world-domination

Stanford to Startup
ecorner.stanford.edu/authorMaterialInfo.html?mid=2735

SERIES GLOSSARY OF KEY TERMS

application: A program that runs on a computer or smartphone. People often call these "apps."

bug: A problem with how a program runs.

byte: A unit of information stored on a computer. One byte is equal to eight digits of binary code—that's eight 1s or 0s.

cloud: Data and apps that are stored on the Internet instead of on your own computer or smartphone are said to be "in the cloud."

data: Information stored on a computer.

debug: Find the problems with an app or program and fix them.

device: Your computer, smartphone, or other piece of technology. Devices can often access the Internet and run apps.

digital: Having to do with computers or stored on a computer.

hardware: The physical part of a computer. The hardware is made up of the parts you can see and touch.

memory: Somewhere that a computer stores information that it is using.

media: Short for multimedia, it's the entertainment or information that can be stored on a computer. Examples of media include music, videos, and e-books.

network: More than one computer or device connected together so information can be shared between them.

pixel: A dot of light or color on a digital display. A computer monitor or phone screen has lots of pixels that work together to create an image.

program: A collection of computer code that does a job.

software: Programs that run on a computer.

technology: Something that people invent to make a job easier or do something new.

INDEX

ABOUT THE AUTHOR

Rosa Waters lives in New York State. She has worked as a writer for several years, producing works on health, history, and other topics.

PICTURE CREDITS

Dreamstime.com:
14: Aprescindere
16: Raluca Tudor
22: Aprescindere
27: GilbertC
32: Piero Cruciatti
36: Kobby Dagan
38: Stanislav Tiplyashin
39: Dolphfyn
40: Lucian Milasan
42: Lucian Milasan
46: Gary Arbach
48: Serban Enache
53: Bevan Goldswain

54: Marcel De Grijs
56: Travelling-light

6: Webby Awards
8: Id Software
10: Daderot
12: King of Hearts
20: Instagram, Inc.
24: Sailko
26: Brian Solis
34: Webby Awards
50: Forbes
51: kawanet | Flickr.com
52: TechCrunch